Watch Your Step

Erin James

BookLeaf
Publishing
India | USA | UK

Presentation by *BookLeaf Publishing*

Web: www.bookleafpub.com

E-mail: info@bookleafpub.com

ISBN: 9789357215091

First edition 2022

ACKNOWLEDGEMENT

Thank you Krista and Karlee, you encourage me to rest when I'm being too hard on myself. Thank you Mommy and Daddy, you encourage me to keep going when I feel I can't take another step. Thank you to the people who live in my house for not completely hating me when I'm too loud (singing or screaming). Thank you to everyone who has sincerely complemented me. Those words keep me going too.

PREFACE

I want to change the world. I want to fix injustice. I want to help people who are hurting. I want everyone to have a chance to experience true joy. I have to figure out me before I can change anything else.

Biology and Circumstances
(December 2022)

When I begin the process
  of separating out
What is part of myself
and what is
    my depression
    or my anxiety
    or my neurodivergence
    or my commitment to someone else
    or my reaction to a stimulus
        based on a previous experience
    or an entirely different factor
        I've yet to discover
            (though I'm attributing it to anxiety)
I begin to get discouraged
At some point it begins to feel
    as if there is nothing left of me
So I adjust the parameters
What do I intentionally incorporate?
To continue to improve, how
    do I apply new information once received?
At what point can I consider myself
    a whole, solid being
    and not just a swarm of
        biology and circumstances?

Life Goals (December 2022)

Goals are like dreams
    I have to make come true
Maybe this is why I short circuit
    every time I try
    to set a goal
I've spent the last four years
    emotionally feeling as if
    every dream I've ever had
    has been taken from me in some way
How do I reach past the pain of losing
    what feels, to me, like everything
    that has ever brought me hope or happiness
    to grasp onto something
    that could bring it back again?

Outline of Me (April 2022)

Once I wrote a poem called Life of Less Than
    I hadn't yet realized I chose
To be the person that designated
    that less than was my prose
It's worse than I had initially thought
    when pitying myself at the time
I'd only been seeing two dimensions
    I'd forgotten that I'm
Living in at least six dimensions
    well actually not literally
I'm facing all directions
    okay let's start with three

There's first the width dimension
    the one that denotes my size
Then we can add height to the mix
    how tall I can see with my eyes
Next will come the dimension of length
    that's how far my feet can go
And time takes up the fourth dimension
    one of the hardest ones to know
I also track my anxiety
    she keeps me on my toes
And then there's my depression
    there's too much he knows

Each one exerts some pressure
    width always wants to be smaller
Height chimes in quickly
    they'd really like to to be taller
Length is constantly fighting
    to pull my feet along
And time quickly gets lost
    in the appealing beat of a song
Anxiety keeps pushing outward
    emptying my inner me
While depression keeps reminding
    I'm not who I want to be

So I pour myself out like mortar
    grinding depression into sand
Hoping with all that I'm made of
    I'll be able to withstand
Becoming an outline of me
    a simple caricature
To bridge gaps that others don't see
    yet keep myself secure

Under (December 2022)

5

underfoot
and underdeveloped
undercover   underground
I've been
   underage
   underprivileged
   undercut
   undervalued
   underrated
   undermined
   undersold
   and underestimated
while undergoing undetermined undertakings
this underdog uncovered
   underlying
   undertones
   underway
ushering in underhanded uneasiness

The under I seem to encounter the least is
    stood

Scarecrow (December 2022)

I traverse this life
    as a person filled with straw
Inconsequential to most
An example when convenient
    but frequently just a face in the crowd

I am one of many
    all possessing the same needs
Desiring similar connections
It's difficult to differentiate
    when zooming out to examine the whole

But let there be a moment
    when I step out of the line
Choose a different course
Achieve a different result
    and suddenly I am examined

Only for this action
    likely only for ridicule
Until they learn that
My head is full of straw
    and I am inconsequential one more

Bootstraps (April 2022)

Don't think you want to live
    vicariously through me
My life hasn't turned out
    the way I wanted it to be

I worked hard to get where I got
    but these bootstraps only pull on my boots
and I'm not proud of decisions to I'd choose
    if you made me do it over again

Because I lived a sheltered life
    but I didn't get to feel safe
and my brain didn't retain
    lessons my parents were trying to make

The only refrain that stayed
    were words that caused pain
Pitting my soul so deeply
    I had to climb out to see the sun again

All the Mes (December 2022)

Personally, when I am writing
    I am writing for all the mes
I'm writing for the me
    that genuinely believed she didn't have a
choice
And I'm writing for the me
    that knows I did and still does now
If I can write for both of them
    then I can feel for both of them
This is one of the reasons for my art
    to feel and heal from the negative emotions
It brings me back to these moments
    but reminds me it's not always one way
When I need now me to remember
    it can still get better
I can write words that mean both

Depression (September 2022)

i am trapped
locked in a room
without a door
the walls advancing
i can no longer afford the space
mortgaged to me at birth
and now it is being foreclosed upon
unable to leave
i am forced to stay
in my memories
picking them apart
desperately searching for a way out
until there's nothing left of me
impotently watching my life
disintegrate before my eyes

Thick Skin (July 2022)

I wasn't blessed with thick skin
    just some sort of emotional regeneration
but it hurts every time
    every comment
        and there are scabs
that never get the chance to heal
    and are torn open each time
the words reach my ears
    and remind my brain
that no matter how many times I hear it
    I feel it
    I know it
    I live it
        and it hurts
wanting desperately to be embraced
    but being terrified of being touched
unable to see a place for myself
    I enjoy the beauty of the people
    as they gather and they mingle
see the joy on their faces

sometimes all I can do is dance at the edge
    and share in the joy
    and move
        my body

       my stupid meat suit
that I love with all my heart
   as best as I can

and be alive

Perfect Timing (August 2022)

Is perfect timing a myth?
   Do some people really have it
or is it gifted periodically
    only to some people
      some of the time?
And if we all had it
    would life be boring?
Or would the world dance?
    For once, feel the feeling
      of absolute joy
        no feelings of being unwanted
        or in the way
          no feelings of needing to
          apologize for your existence
Sometimes I think that is what
    loving myself feels like:
        Perfect Timing

When There Are Few Words
(December 2022)

sometimes poetry eludes me
the words won't come
kept behind a dam
building up
swelling into a nappe
but only a few trickle over
the failure insufficient
to provide relief
to the exsiccated pen
eagerly awaiting release

Imposter Syndrome (August 2022)

The imposter syndrome is strong
    I was raised to see things
    from other people's perspectives
The drive to deny myself
    and aspire to understand
    why this bad thing
       happening to me
Is justified
    because it is understandable

It's driven me almost crazy
    searching in all directions
       to find a way out
         to find a place
           to find...   something
that helps me feel
    that it is okay
       to take off the mask
         to express my rage
         to defend that person
that HAD to understand while they were in pain
and couldn't to do anything about it in the
moment

Emotions (August 2022)

I am not sure how I feel
    about feeling my emotions
They're dangerous
    roiling under the surface
They have the capacity
    to halt progress
        in the middle of anything
    to cause reactions
        that can injure
    to pressure the beginning
        of something before it needs to start
    to create a sense of euphoria
        too difficult to leave
    to attach to someone
        who should be left alone
    to leave someone
        when they most needed help
    to run until
        all of the muscles are exhausted
    to curl into a small space
        until the threat has passed
They attach meaning
    sometimes after
    sometimes before
    sometimes during

    sometimes accurately
    sometimes unfairly
    sometimes false
they don't care about morals or truth or anything
really
    except for themselves
Anger and fear for protection
Love and happiness to keep going
Comfort to come in and calm the other ones
I do know I can't picture
    living my life without them

Star Walker (May 2003)

She draws stars on her feet
to keep her occupied
her bit of heaven
to walk about on Earth
but walking on stars
won't get her anywhere
beautiful lost Star Walker

Her head in the clouds
her heart in the sky
her voice on the wind
her feet in the stars
but walking on stars
won't get her anywhere
beautiful lost Star Walker

The dance to nowhere
beckons to her ears
spinning in circles
around, around in the stars
but walking on stars
won't get her anywhere
beautiful lost Star Walker

Joy (December 2022)

They sing in the shower
    and when doing dishes
They are delighted by beauty
    and uniqueness
They always wanted to be beautiful
    but they never trusted their eyes
    when they looked in a mirror
They love to dance
    but feel ashamed of their body
    and aren't sure how to move it
They like to pretend they are a
    ballerina when they think
    no one is watching
Oh! You should see them
    in the moments when the anxiety leaves
    when they forget to feel shame
When they get lost in a thought
    or the rhythm of a song
    and the joy shines on their face

They're Dancing (December 2022)

They're skipping again

There's a lightness to their step
    that's been missing for a long time

I can tell they don't trust it.

But in those moments
    when their anxiety is distracted
When they get caught up in an idea
    and they forget to behave...

That's when their feet begin to dance

Morning Routine (December 2022)

The curve of their arm
    they glide lotion on their skin
    entices and delights me
    the motion steady and deliberate
I catch a glimpse of them
    in the mirror
    as they bend to
    massage the moisture in
They don't see their beauty enough

Something comes to mind that
    amuses them and a smile
    forms at the corner
    of their sweet mouth
And the laugh lines
    they sometimes worry about
    show prominently at
    the corners of their eyes
I am struck speechless for a moment.

They are radiant!

I love Erin (December 2022)

I love her... I'm sorry, I mean them.
I love them.
I mean... Erin.
I love Erin.
I... oh this is awkward.
How do I put this down on paper?
It's felt so inappropriate to say
    for so very long.
I don't even know how to write it,
    but she is my favorite.
er... they're my favorite.
Erin's my favorite.
The words are clumsy.
It still feels strange to say.
I'm still figuring out the best way
    to do it.
I'll probably get it wrong a lot.
Fortunately, I have the rest
    of their life to keep trying
    to get it right.
I love you, Erin.

Schrödinger's Friend

every time I say goodbye to someone
    they die
only metaphorically usually but the sentiment
    is real
until I interact with them again they are
    Schrödinger's Friend
they exist both vibrantly alive and as
    only memory

so if I think of someone
    I know
when I am alone and not
    actively interacting
that person is nothing more than
    the memories
I choose to hold of them within
    my mind

this can be utterly freeing
    or condemning
depending on the criteria I use
    to determine
which of the memories to pour out
    into view
and which memories I choose to keep back and

let fade

sometimes this process is easy
    to do
either there are too few memories and I use
    them all
or there are so very many to
    choose from
I can assemble a bouquet of only the
    best ones

the trouble I run into when I am
    all alone
and visiting with my many
    Schrödinger's Friends
is the memories I recall of me tend to
    inevitably bad
and devastatingly pale to
    the others

until I am the one dead

Dear One (December 2022)

Hello Dear One
It's been awhile
    since you looked in the mirror
    and realized
    you loved what you saw
Rest with me a moment
    and reflect
This world's rough
    It doesn't stop to wait
    for anyone
    especially you
But you don't have to ride
    every ride

Sweet Dear One
Remember that
    you still love the person that
    smiles at you
    opposite the glass
You still gaze in awe at
    who you've become
There is still pride
    in how hard you've worked to
    finally love that
    fickle outward shell

You're improving daily
    Remember that

I still love you, Dear One.

Life of Less Than (June 2019)

What does it mean
    to live a life of less than?
How do you go
    through each and every day?
What do you do
    to live a life of less than?
Can you figure out
    how you managed to get this way?

Did you feel too responsible?
Were you rejected when you were young?
Did you grow up too fast?
Did you fail to hold your tongue?

It's hard to believe
    you started out this way.
So who determined less than
    would be your day to day?

www.ingramcontent.com/pod-product-compliance
Lightning Source LLC
Chambersburg PA
CBHW070725160726
48003CB00006BA/2376